Hidden Mysteries of the Honeybee

by

Deborah Lynne Flanegan

Hidden Mysteries of the Honeybee
by Deborah Lynne Flanegan

Printed in the United States of America

ISBN 978-1-60791-385-6

www.xulonpress.com

Dedication

This book is dedicated in loving memory to my father, Howard L. Ellard, who went to be with the Lord, May 1998. He also had a passion to delve into scripture in order to have a greater understanding of God's Word, and He always told me to, "Never be afraid to ask a question." And also to my husband of 41 Years, Ken, who has been very supportive of my love to spend time in biblical research and teaching projects. Neither one of these men could be classified as a drone.

Table of Contents

Introduction

Over thirty years ago while studying the Bible I came to realize that every word had a meaning and many had hidden meanings if you cared enough to do some research. The first word that intrigued me was almond.

Why did God use the almond blossom and knobs as the design for the menorah in the tabernacle?

Why did God have Aaron's rod bud, bloom and produce the fruit of an almond, as a sign of who was to be the high priest?

Why was the branch that God showed to Jeremiah in Jeremiah 1:11 an almond branch?

After some simple investigation I found the Hebrew word for almond and watch are both from the same Hebrew root word meaning "to watch over." So there seemed to be a connection between the menorah being the only light provided inside the Holy Place (a type of Christ, Who is the Light of the World) and the High Priest (also a type of Christ) as the one who watches over the spiritual needs of Israel. I'm sure there is more to be revealed about this type/symbol of the almond but I got side tracked with looking for other words that were only in the Bible a few times and the next one just happened to be the bee.

It was during the 1980's when the Holy Spirit impressed me with the idea of writing a book about the bee. But in 1984 while being very involved with Right to Life and being an elected delegate in the political arena, my plans soon were curtailed due to a much-unexpected pregnancy. (Having two sons 16 years between them.) And so I never wrote the book, only a short paper on the bee and honey.

It wasn't until 2007, while at a Women's Spring Retreat; one of the other speakers mentioned to me a vision she had had the night before. Part of it showed me dressed in a long purple robe, with something shiny bright (not jewelry) wrapped around my throat (vocal cords). People were gathering around to learn what I was teaching. Then she said, "You have a honeycomb in your hand and your mouth is dripping with honey." The statement startled me as I then remembered what the Lord had impressed me to do 30 years ago, to write a book about the bee and honey. This time I followed through with the "suggestion."

CHAPTER 1

Why a Book About a Bee?

Whyaboutabookaboutabee?

Whyabookaboutabee? That just seems to roll off the tongue doesn't it? Whyabookaboutabee? Boy, where do I start? And what do I mean by hidden mysteries?

As my name is Deborah, which in Hebrew means Bee or Seeking One, (I like to think of myself as the seeker of truth and sweetness) so you can understand my natural curiosity with the bee.

Bees are mentioned only four times in the Bible and all are in the Old Testament. Nothing really interesting in that except for one passage, (Isaiah 7:19 NASB) records that the Lord whistled for the bee. But up until recently, scientists didn't know if bees even had the ability to hear, but God knew.

The honeybee has to be one of God's most complicated and fascinating creatures of all time. Every element of the aerodynamic honeybee boggles the mind. *"For as the heavens are higher than the earth, so are my ways higher than your ways and my thoughts than your thoughts."* (Isaiah 55: 9 NKJ)

Isn't it amazing how God in all His magnificent knowledge devised a way that whoever reads His Word for even the first time would be able to understand the simple plan of salvation? And then later you come to realize that He built into the Holy Scriptures layer upon layer of knowledge hidden within the words and phrases used to show forth the <u>foreshadowing</u> of things to come. Such as: types and shadows of the Messiah, the Church, the rapture and actually the total prophetic view of history to the end of the age.

> *"For Christ is the end of the Law (the limit at which it ceases to be, for the Law leads up to Him who is the fulfillment of its <u>types</u>, and in Him the purpose which it was designed to accomplish is fulfilled. That is, the purpose of the Law is fulfilled in Him) as the means of righteousness (right relationship to God) for everyone who trusts in and adheres to and relies on Him."*(Romans 9:4 AMP)

> *"For whatever was thus written in former days, was written for our instruction, that by our steadfast and patient endurance and the encouragement (drawn) from the scriptures we might hold fast to and cherish hope."* (Romans 15:4 AMP)

The Old Testament is the New Testament concealed and the New Testament is the Old Testament revealed. That old saying certainly is true.

Every word in the Holy Scriptures was engineered to fit perfectly, even those words mentioned only a few times. We are told that it is God breathed, which means it is alive and His spirit (breath) is in the very Word that is written. No matter how deep we research His Word, we will never comprehend the totality of His infinite intelligence.

We can only get a glimpse of His superiority as we feast upon the sights: the grandeur of the mountains, or a simple trickling waterfall. Look at the various leaf designs, watch a crisp clear little trout stream gently moving along, leaving little bits of sand granules shimmering in the bottom of the stream; or inhale the fragrance of luscious damp black soil so full of the nutrients needed to sustain the life-giving abundance of a seed. Rejoice in the soft spring winds brushing your cheek or the invigorating winter air being so cold you can feel the sharp ice crystals as you inhale slowly feeling the "breath of God" invade your lungs. What a rush! Experience the CRACK of lightening and the deep powerful rumbling of thunder as it shakes the ground and vibrates through the air.

Well, the honeybee is also a creative wonder to behold. Only the Divine Supreme Being of the Universe could have thought up these little black and yellow "Bundles of Buzz."

Mankind has not ignored the sweet richness of the honeybees' labor, dedication, industrial drive, or paradoxical ability to fly. Many ancient cultures considered the bee a deity and associated it with hidden wisdom. (They certainly have the hidden wisdom part correct.)

Aristotle (384 – 322 BC) wrote, "Each bee on her return is followed by three or four companions.... How they do it has not yet been observed."

Carolus Linnaeus gave the honeybee its scientific name of Apis melifera L. in 1758. It literally means "the honey-carrying bee", then in 1761 a more descriptive name, A. mellifica, or "the honey-making bee" was proposed. Although the name was more accurate in describing what the bee does, scientific nomenclature dictated that the earlier name be retained.

In 1973 Karl von Frisch gave his Nobel Lecture "Decoding the Language of the Bee" in which he stated, "Some 60 years ago, many biologists thought that bees were totally color blind animals." It was in 1923 that Karl had discovered the honeybee not only could see colors but also had a "language of dance."

Soon after the end of World War II in war-ravaged Germany, Karl von Frisch was observing the dance of bees and "reading" the language he himself had deciphered.

By 1973 his experiments had shown that they not only communicate in this language but they could transmit the direction and distance to the flowers, by using the polarization of the sunrays. At this time the "waggle dance" was also discovered, "This straight stretch is sharply marked by tail-wagging dance movements and simultaneously toned (in the true meaning of the word) by a buzzing sound."

CHAPTER 2

Hidden Mysteries

Types/Shadows or Symbols

What are the "hidden mysteries" all about? All scholars recognize that God uses types and shadows to hide His mysteries. The tabernacle of Moses in Exodus Chapters 25-40 was patterned after the heavenly temple. The Passover lamb in Exodus is a perfect picture of Christ as the Lamb of God who would suffer and die at the Jewish Passover season. *"...and He who reveals **mysteries** has made known to you what will take place."* (Daniel 2:29 NKJ) *"To me, the very least of all saints, this grace was given, to preach to the Gentiles the unfathomable riches of Christ, and to bring to light what is the administration of the mystery which for ages has been hidden in God who created all things; so that the manifold wisdom of God might now be made known through the church to the rulers and the authorities in the heavenly places."* (Ephesians 3:8-10 NKJ)

Let me give you some background to help you understand what is meant by type/shadow or symbol.

A type or shadow is a prophetic image, of one object foreshadowing another, while a symbol is just one item standing for something else but with no prophetic quality to it.

In the writing of Holy Scripture, God caused the recording of history to be put in such a way that certain persons were seen as prefiguring or **foreshadowing** another person to come.

In Genesis 37-50 it tells of Joseph's life which foreshadows many types/shadows of Jesus' life: A firstborn son, miracle birth, beloved son, a shepherd, rejected by brethren, sold for silver, falsely accused etc.

The beasts of the earth, the fowls of heaven, the fish of the sea and the earth... (Job 12: 7-8 NKJ) - are all speaking a message to mankind. Each has their distinctive traits, characteristics and nature; whether positive or negative and man may learn numerous lessons from such.

These creatures, created by God, teach much truth when used by God for symbolic purposes. *"It is for the glory of God to conceal a thing."* (Proverbs 25:2 NKJ)

We must be aware that there is no such thing as a "perfect type," because of the very nature of things used as types were all marked with flaws and incompleteness. But God had to use the flawed and the inadequate created things to point towards Christ, Who is the undefiled, unblemished, and Perfect One.

Within the type/shadow or symbol is hidden truth to be discovered by those who wish to seek it out. As we venture on, let's discover more about God's magnificent creation. As we do, we'll find a hidden mystery showing how we as the "Body of Christ" (Bride of Christ without spot or wrinkle) was meant to function.

Ecclesiastes 1:9 NKJ states *"that which has been is what will be, that which is done is what will be done."*

CHAPTER 3

Bundles of Buzz

It begins...

A bee places a tiny dollop of food in the bottom of each six-sided cell in the brood chamber of the honeycomb, the queen waddles by depositing in it a pearly white egg. "Well, that was number 1,778! Can someone rub my back? PLEASE!"

Three days later a teeny tiny grub-like larva crawls out of the egg, but remains in the "bassinet." These "baby bees" are then fed over a thousand times a day. (We thought every two hours was bad!)

Five days later the larva (toddler) hatches and the other bees (nursery workers) place a wax cap over its "crib." (Naptime.) Inside the cell, the larva spins a cocoon, actually weaves its own SILK "blanket" and changes into a pupa (teenager.) A mysterious metamorphosis with all of its intricate chemical changes takes place in the body of this tiny creature.

After 21 days of gestation this sterile adult female honeybee stripes off her larval skin, "that was waaay too tight!" and nibbles her way out of the cell without any assistance. Boy is she motivated. Being such a meticulous housekeeper, she immediately jumps in (with all six feet) and begins cleaning up her "bedroom" without ever having been taught what to do. Once that is completed, the multi-talented bee becomes a bona-fide card-carrying member of the colony - Local Hive # 7. "Hi Ho, Hi Ho, It's off to work we go..." But wait until you see what all that entails?

CHAPTER 4

You Are What You Eat

Royalty, Slave or Court Jester

Your Menu Choices Are:

Royal Jelly Supreme: Fit for a queen. A luscious five-days of being literally bathed in a "tub" of royal jelly until you mature into a fully developed female queen bee. (Sounds like Esther as she was being prepared for the king – must have something to do with royalty.) You will continue this lavish spread for the remainder of your life. Thus being so filled with royal jelly, you will be capable of starting your own hive to further the "hivedom."

Steak and Salad Special: As a <u>fertilized</u> egg you eat a healthy balance of protein and energy. This 48-hours of all you can eat royal jelly buffet is followed with three days of "homemade" beebread, which will cause you to be transformed into an adult sterile female (worker or neutral) bee. You will continue feasting on beebread, which allows you to provide "mother's milk" (royal jelly) to those in need of it. Once you leave the "nanny's area" you will eat exclusively honey.

Death by Honey: A two-day banquet of royal jelly followed with three days of homemade beebread and you (the <u>unfertilized</u> egg) will be changed into a fully equipped male bee at which time you will chow down exclusively on honey; pure and sweet but not a balanced meal, especially for those who do not exercise. "Oh dear, I'm under conviction now. I'll be sure and start my exercise routine tomorrow."

Queen Bee
Her Supreme Majesty, Ruler Over
Local Hive #7

The queen basically is the mother of all the other bees in the hive and the only one to lay eggs. She lays her weight in eggs everyday, 1,500-2,000 of them! During the months of April and May she will lay eggs around the clock as no youngsters are raised during the winter months. It takes about 20 seconds for each egg to be "birthed." (Poor little thing, I hope it's easy labor.) Each egg is approximately the size of the dot (tittle) over this "i." She is equipped to retain sufficient sperm from her several drones (consorts) to lay fertilized eggs for three to five years, even though she may only live as little as one year.

"Her royal highness" continually emits a pheromone, exclusive to her (maybe she should bottle and sell it, Elizabeth Taylor did pretty well), which lets the other bees in her hive know her locality at all times. (She certainly doesn't need to get trampled on in the dark.) This particular attractive substance/ aroma is removed from her body and shared among all the workers. Her entourage (ladies in waiting who surround the queen in order to assist with her continuous feeding, grooming and protection,) if needed can tell how close she is to them by her scent. Remember all this is happening in the pitch-black darkness of the hive.

This scent/pheromone composition is quite sophisticated in that the aroma of the queen governs the personality of the entire colony. "A little dab behind the antennae and under the wings, I think that will do it." It has the properties to communicate to the hive, "Don't be anxious for nothing, for I am here and still on the throne." Thus helping to keep them calm, docile and reassured that all is well. It's disastrous to get them riled up or confused. This scent will also suppress lady workers from laying unfertilized eggs (male honeybees) or building queen cells which would only drain their precious supply of "liquid gold."

Her ladyship walks (or should I say drags herself) around all day laying eggs. That's all, just laying eggs! But ladies, can you imagine being nine months pregnant and in labor your whole life? I wonder if any of her royal guards ever give her a foot massage, talk about swollen feet!

Worker Bee
"Girl, they sure have named you right!
Workaholic or what! Can you say, 'slave!'"

While this fertilized egg is developing in its clois-
tered cell she is surrounded and supported by great
quantities of food. She emerges all soft and downy
but incapable of making wax, stinging or flying for a
short time. Worker bee, what a dull name for such a
prolific task oriented bee, I think she at least deserves
to be called Princess, Aunt Bea or something.

This undersized sterile female is a dynamo during
her brief life. First thing she does upon leaving her
"room" is to make sure the cell is left immaculately
clean. She's likened to the woman who must pickup
and clean everything before the housekeeper comes.
"Suzy homemaker" continues to care for the "young-
lings", helps to build honeycomb, and takes care of
nectar, etc. "You go girl!" This "big sister" is now
referred to as a house bee or nursery worker, and she
does all this with no instructions or training. Inherent
knowledge?

Her metamorphous (climb up the corporate
ladder) is relative to the bee's age "temporal poly-
theism" as she advances in her duties she moves
closer to the hive's exit and out into the big wide
wonderful world of color where danger lurks around
every bush and tree.

While still a house bee she races ahead of the
queen to prepare empty cells for the pearly white
eggs, or follows after the queen feeding the ever-
hungry grubs. Later the always-efficient nursemaid

will cap the cells when the larva's feeding time expires and the "rug rats" need to start their molting process by "crocheting" their own cocoons.

When the "teeny boppers" emerge they spend only 40% of their time working. That leaves 60% of the time that they stand around the honeycomb ready to engage in any activity that's needed. Sort of sounds like our teenagers, standing at the sidelines of life waiting for the keys to the car.

The worker/forager bee lives barely six weeks during the busy summer, but several months during the fall, winter, and spring when there is less work to do. Honeybees remain active throughout the winter months consuming honey (high energy drink) to prevent them from freezing to death.

A single speck of honey (high-octane fuel) gives the "feather-weight flier" power enough to float from flower to flower for a quarter of a mile. The bee must fill up her tank with honey (liquid gold—That's what we think of fuel now too!) exactly the right amount to get her to the source of all her needs and back home again. If a mistake is made, she will not be able to return.

This little warrior's barbed sting and associated venom sac is modified so when it pulls free of her delicately striped body, the sting apparatus has its own musculature and ganglion which allows it to keep pumping in the venom once detached from the "business" end of the bee. The "girls" will only sting when they feel the hive is in danger. She literally gives her life for the safety of the home. This velvety tiger-striped body conceals a hidden "eye of the tiger" when it comes to protecting her own.

Defense against other insects is usually accomplished through surrounding the intruder with a mass of warrior bees who vibrate their muscles, by contracting flight muscles without moving their wings, so vigorously that it raises the temperature of the <u>intruder to a lethal level</u>. I can just see their little heads getting red and steam pouring out of their antennae. Their actions cause destruction of the enemy without using any physical intervention that would automatically kill them in the process. How about that for effective spiritual warfare?

Several "patrol officers" walk the beat at the entrance to the honeycomb chamber and smell every bee that enters, as every hive has their own distinctive pheromone. Sort of like drug sniffing dogs at customs. Any creature not belonging to the nest is not permitted entrance with the exception of drones, as they are welcome in any hive as insurance against emergency situations.

At the age of 10 – 20 days old she is known as a forager or field bee. Now this little "scout" (she must be a Girl Scout as they too carry and deliver sweet stuff – cookies!) in her first time outside of the hive she will take short practice flights in front of the colony on warm afternoons to acquaint her with the appearance and immediate vicinity of the hive. The term "play flights" has been given to this activity because the bee bobs and weaves in the air while facing the hive.

She will then begin flying to the meadows for collection of pollen, (the source of protein) and nectar (the source of energy) for her entire hive. Becoming one great little shopper, with her tools safety tucked away to collect the produce in her environmentally friendly baskets and storage tank, (no plastic bags here) bringing home the best of the groceries. She will no longer do any housework. ("Freedom! She's got the car keys and she's not staying homebound anymore – "yard sales here I come.")

This "lady scout" will do an extremely accurate investigation of the landscape for miles in every direction and bring back a detailed report on the prospects of nectar. Perhaps a dozen "girls" will leave the cluster and fly off in various directions, just browsing around in the vicinity of the hive in ever-widening circles.

How these "elixir detectives" communicate the destination of the source of nectar and pollen to other anxiously awaiting "shoppers" in the hive may be the most ingenious and multifaceted form of social behavior existing outside of the human race. They will defy the laws of simplicity in order to relay the life and death information to the others. This information includes the exact species that is ripe for the picking, a compass bearing for the direction, the distance to the "angelic ambrosia" and the quantity available! "Attention Ladies! Lovely red flowers just dripping with nectar – that a way!"

Wait a minute! We are talking about little fluffy critters with a brain the size of a pinhead. How can they learn such information or impart it to others? Is God great or what!!

She will frequently fly (you guessed it, that qualifies her as a Frequent Flier) over 400 miles, actually wearing out her fabulous gossamer wings to the point where flying is no longer an option. At that time, five to six weeks into her short life span, the "flier extraordinaire" will walk away from the hive, thus no longer being a burden to the colony. She dies shortly thereafter, but she leaves a legacy just as Enoch did. *"So all the days of Enoch were three hundred sixty and five years: And Enoch walked with God: and he was not for God took him."* (Genesis 5:23-24 NKJ)

The demure worker bee is a great picture of the woman in Proverbs 31:13 - 23 – (*Italics mine*)

13. She looks for wool (*nectar*) and flax (*Pollen*) and works with her hands (*6 hairy legs*) in delight. 14. She is like merchant ships (*zeppelins*); She brings her food from afar. (*Nectar can be very far away.*) 15. She rises also while it is still night and gives food to her household and portions to her maidens (*in the darkness of the hive*). 16. She considers a field (*of flowers*) and buys it (*tells everyone about it;*) from her earnings she plants a vineyard (*makes honey*). 17. She girds herself with strength (stinger) and makes her arms strong (*with energy from the honey*). 18. She senses that her gain is good; (*gets the highest quality of nectar.*) Her lamp does not go out at night. 19. She stretches out her hands to the distaff, and her hands grasp the spindle (*making silk and lines of resin*). 20. She extends her hand to the poor, and she stretches out her hands to the needy (*drones*). 21. She is not afraid (*no fear*) of the snow for her house-

hold, for all her household is clothed with scarlet. (*honey is stored away for the winter months and able to apply fuzzy wallpaper to the walls as needed.*) 22. She makes coverings for herself (*silk cocoon*); Her clothing is fine linen and purple (*yellow and black — yellow speaks of humility*). 23. Her husband is known in the gates, when he sits among the elders of the land. (*Sits is the operative word.*)

Although the honeybee is referred to as being black and yellow in color they are actually more honey colored – and like honey they vary from light yellow to a darker rusty orange color.

Drone The Slow Moving Dirigible
Alias: Buzzy Blimp or Hurly Burly Bee!

These male honeybees result from unfertilized eggs. They are extremely clumsy, lethargic and unkempt critters, approximately twice the size of the "lovely ladies." The boys are lackadaisical in their attitude and don't do much for themselves. They can't even get out of their own cells without help from the "nursery" bees. (They have to be prodded out of bed!) They are totally dependent on the worker bees, which even have to feed them! "Hey, Honey when's dinner?" After the first few days the guys start helping themselves to stored honey. ("Oh, No! He's found the food stash!") It's the "sanitation" bees that have to continually remove the drone's waste in order to keep the hive as sterile as a hospital's surgical unit.

A conspicuous brush of hairs is visible at the end of the bee's blunt abdomen. His genitals (hey, I'm trying to be very tactful here,) are actually folded up inside of his abdomen making his final physical act of mating an exhaustive experience, using all his strength and energy to release his endophallus in order to fertilize the queen. His reproductive organs and associated abdominal tissues are literally ripped from his body at mating. (Circumcision gone a muck. That's gotta hurt!)

If you compare the drone proportionally to other animals, the size of his genitalia is among the largest of any animal on earth. (I know when to keep quiet.)

The guys' only function in the world of the honeybee is to mate with a queen. Usually in the early afternoon they survey the area while flying about 30-50 feet in the air searching for available virgin bees. The "macho macho man" cruises from hive to hive and the "boys" also have drone congregations located a good distance from any bee colonies. (Drone congregations? It's just another name for the local pool hall where the "safari hunters" play billiards and compare the size of their antennae. Of course they refer to them as antlers—it sounds more masculine—I figure it must be a guy thing!) They are the only honeybees allowed to wander from one colony to another without getting into trouble with the "security guards." It is still unknown how these congregational areas are established but we do know they exist.

The male bee's most striking feature is their enormous eyes. (Isn't that just like a man?) Really, the "guys" have to have great eyesight to make sure they do not lose track of a destined-to-be queen as she flies approximately 100 feet up into the sky during the "nuptial" flight. Picture them all standing around the lamppost in front of the pool hall with their hairy hands raised to their foreheads shading their eyes from the glare of the sun gazing up with delirious anticipation.

Drones have no stinger, no electromagnetic charge to attract pollen, and are allergic to work! Any "gents" that are left by the end of the season are considered non-essential and driven out of the "assembly" to die. As winter approaches the "undertaker" bees remove developing drones from their cells and begin to harass the "good old boys" first. Rarely do the worker bees sting the drones but the "guys" are pushed and pulled so much that it is difficult for the drones to eat, which is about all they want to do. When the situation warrants, these "dainty darlings" (worker bees) will take extreme measures and show phenomenal power-lifting skills. The little so called underdeveloped female bee, which is half the size of the drone, will literally pick up the "hefty guys" and toss them out of the hive. Then the "police" on guard duty will prevent them from re-entering.

It is very essential to the rest of the "tribe" to remove the non-workers during the winter months. The "hivedom" can't allow those who do not work to eat up the rations previously put away for storage, if the drones were allowed to stay the whole hive would starve. It's interesting that Webster's 9th Colligate Dictionary states the meaning of Drone is: One who lives on the labors of others or a deep sustained or monotonous sound—HUM.

A drone's life span is 90 days. In all fairness, a drone does not have the mouthparts or equipment to do the work of the female bees. They are only capable of doing one other thing, and that's helping with the heating and cooling maintenance of the hive. Scientists are still trying to figure out if the drone may be of value to the colony, perhaps by affecting the morale of the colony or in other ways that are still not understood at this time. (Maybe he is real good at giving compliments? "Whoa! Gracie, you look great!" Or maybe he would make a funny court jester?)

CHAPTER 5

Pomp and Circumstance

Battle Cry

If a colony wants to swarm or needs to replace a failing queen, the old queen will lay several eggs destined to become "royalty" in special vertically hung cells, 25 mm in length. But if an emergency arises and there is no queen available to lay an egg in the "royal" chamber then the worker bee, (in some mysterious way yet to be discovered) selects a regular worker grub less than three days old to become a queen.

They will then modify that horizontal cell to make room for the extended size needed for a queen bee. Five and a half days after hatching the virgin queen larva becomes a pupa, and sixteen days after that, she emerges as an adult. At which time she will only lay drone eggs until she has mated. The arrangement is perfect.

The worker bees practically ignore the young innocent queen as long as there is a laying queen in the hive. However, they very quickly are attracted to her and begin to feed and groom her. Within the first few days the "little workout gurus" also use pinching and biting to encourage the naive queen to get physically fit in order to go on her "wedding" flight. Can't you just see her decked out in a lovely soft yellow sweat suit, white "tennies" with shocking electric neon lemon laces, and an adorable yellow polka dot sweatband around her head just jogging along while her "trainers" come right behind her ready to bite her in the ... fanny if she slows down!

After about a week of this forced exercise routine "Miss Queen" is agile and physically ready for the mating flight. She will leave between noon and 4 p.m. flying a considerable distance from the hive to visit the drone's congregational area where the mating generally takes place. How she knows where to find the drones is another unsolved mystery. The fully developed queen then has a mating "nuptial" flight up to 100 feet in the air with as many as 20 drones. After fertilization she will either:

(1.) Return to the hive a half-hour later (not much of a honeymoon) ready to lay worker bee eggs for the rest of her life,

(2.) Or she will fight to the death the older queen.

Often the older queen wisely leaves taking a part of the bees with her instead, but this can only be accomplished by starving the old queen in order for her to be capable of flying again. (Get out those yellow "sweats" again. It's workout time.)

At swarming time, the hive becomes highly energized. It's moving day! All work stops and out of the hive swooshes a terrifying ball of 35,000 or more bees. The scouts in that swarm are sent out to find a location for a new hive. The mating flight of the queen does not occur until the "scouts" return to the waiting bees, and the entire swarm has moved to the new location.

When two queens fight, they are able to sting repeatedly, as they have no barb on their stinger and can easily pull it out and sting again. When the fight begins one or both queens will often sound a high, clear note as a "battle cry." The sound is made in anger by forcing air through ten little holes (spiracles) in the side of the queen's body. The sound is a signal to the entire hive for everyone to stand back and wait for a single queen to emerge. (It's interesting that Ten is the number symbolizing law and order.)

If the new queen decides to stay in the hive she will locate the other cells with potential queens and kill them by stinging them through the wax walls of their cells, that is another reason she was created with a stinger that can be used repeatedly.

At times the old failing queen and her young daughter may continue to live and lay eggs in the same colony for a considerable period of time.

CHAPTER 6

Can You Recognize a Drone When You See One?

Remote poised for action...

Right from the start, I want to make sure that you do not, <u>DO NOT</u>, classify the drones as men and the worker bees as women! That **type** doesn't fly (excuse the pun but couldn't help it). So just get that right out of your head, even though I have to admit it is pretty funny.

Can't you just visualize this in cartoon form; the drone as an obese, disheveled and unkempt bee with his bulging (honey-filled) belly protruding out from his dingy tee shirt and slightly too tight pants with the top button undone; a can of "Honey Dew" in his hand, lounging on the couch with the TV remote poised for action and a cigar dangling out of the corner of his mouth, yelling, "Hey Honey, get me another Dew!

"BELCH"... just not a pretty picture, certainly not what we would think of as Christ like.

But wait a minute! The drone does resemble what I refer to as a quote-unquote "Christian." The Christian that thinks he is fine just shuffling along, never really understanding or having a relationship with the Father, assuming that because he's a good guy and may have accepted the Lord once a long time ago, that's all he needs. That refers to **both genders, male and female** not just men! Remember Galatians 3:28, *"There is neither Jew nor Greek, there is neither slave nor free man, there is neither male nor female; for you are all one in Christ Jesus."*

I struggled with trying to understand why there seemed to be two very different types of believers in the fellowship. When mediating on this one morning in my time with the Lord, He revealed the following to me:

(1.) We can either live in the world as a spiritual being

(2.) Or, we can be a spiritual being living in the world!

There is a huge difference. We are to be in the world, not of it. I know you have heard this a hundred times, but where is your focus, World or Spirit?

In (1.) we live our lives, being parents, children, employees, executives, laboring in OUR endeavors, maybe to be used of God here or there to occasionally further the kingdom, teach a class, lead someone to Christ, give to the poor etc., while carrying on a somewhat personal relationship with Jesus Christ (a long distance one at that) while taking care of the world's necessities and wants, hoping all the while to live a comfortable life here and now, with the guarantee of a future heavenly home.

Or (2.) living (dwelling) in Him where we are immersed or so absorbed with His presence we exude (ooze out) Jesus while we carry out our physical lives, being lead of the Holy Spirit in all that we say and do. That reminds me of the queen's pheromone that is secreted from her body at all times. Jesus said, "I do only what I see my Father doing." You too will see the world in a whole new light if you're looking through His eyes. I think Paul referred to this in Ephesians 3:16-21 (NASB) *"That He would grant you according to the riches of His glory, to be strengthened with might by <u>His Spirit in the inner man;</u> that Christ may dwell in your hearts by faith; that you being <u>rooted and grounded in love</u>, may be able to comprehend (with all saints) what is the breadth, and length, and depth, and height and to know the love of Christ, which passes knowledge; and that you might be filled with all the fullness of God."*

THE DIFFERENCE?

Joy — *OR* — **Jubilation** (Great Joy — Joy
Unspeakable)
Fear — *OR* — **Suspense or Anticipation of
the glorious unknown**

Reverence — *OR* — **Awesomeness of His presence**
Wonder — *OR* — **Intimately knowing Him as Adam knew Eve**
Human Frailty — *OR* — **Spiritual strength beyond belief** (I can do all things through Christ)

Remember, the Father's presence is available to all through Christ Jesus. It was at the time of Christ's sacrifice for us on the cross; that the veil, which separated the Holy of Holies from the Holy Place in the Jewish temple, was torn from top to bottom. This veil was the thickness of a man's hand and 60 feet tall; no human hands could have torn it. Thus, God Himself gave us access to His very throne room through the Blood of Christ, which set in motion the New Covenant.

We're talking <u>sanctification</u> here. That's the difference between the "Christian" (those who accept Christ as Savior but never really set themselves apart from the world unto God in holiness) and the true believer walking in a right relationship with the Father. Until recently, I never really understood the act of sanctification. I just took it for granted that everyone, upon asking the Lord to forgive them and to come into their life, automatically was aware they were entering into a covenant agreement with God and making the decision to step out of the world and into that invisible Kingdom of God (walking in a new way, living in holiness).

But now I can see clearly the difference. It's like the honeybee dangling precariously by one itsy-bitsy claw from the edge of a petal, just barely holding on, making it into heaven by the tip of a toenail. Unless you're a honeybee I wouldn't recommend it. But don't you want the abundant life, and the blessings that God wants to pour out on you?

When the road of life gets a little bumpy, it's the "Christian" who will be whining, complaining and murmuring about the situation, seeking others to pray for them and a shoulder to cry on. Not really wanting to take the time and/or effort themselves to be abiding in His presence. They desire to have all the blessings but have no aspiration to fulfill their part of the covenant. Salvation is freely given— Blessings are conditional upon keeping the vows of the covenant (marriage contract). You will notice in reading Scripture that it's some of the smallest words that hold the key to understanding the verse, little words such as; if, and, but, (they should cause a red flag to pop-up in your mind) that this promise or blessing is only available if you honor your part of the covenant.

Read Deuteronomy 28 (The Blessings and Cursing) that explains it very well. If you obey my word...I will do...etc.

These "Christians" are as unbalanced as the drones, who are in the hive but don't participate in anything unless their life is in jeopardy. They are ambling around lopsided in their spirit. And like the drones that visit among the hives and congregate with other drones, the "Christians" drift from church to church and teaching to teaching, (always seeking His hand but not His face) never putting down roots. They find it difficult or just not worth the time and effort to continue gathering together with the believers. *"This is the man who hears the word and immediately receives it with joy; yet he has no firm root in himself, but is only temporary, and when affliction or persecution arises because of the Word, immediately he falls away. And the one on who seed was sown among the thorns, this is the man who hears the word, and the worry of the world and the deceitfulness of wealth choke the word, and it becomes unfruitful."* (Matthew: 13: 20-22 NASB)

Like the house bees who take care of the mess left behind by the drones, it's the Christians who are growing in the faith and walking with the Lord who take care of the discontentment, disagreements, back biting, flames of dispute and friendly fire within the camp that the "Christians" leave behind as they flitter from place to place, trying to find a congregation that is tailored to fit their wants. "Oh, I like it here; I can be more myself and not have to change my life style at all. They love me just the way I am, who needs all that spiritual stuff, that just takes too much of my free time!"

Don't get me wrong, true believers also have trials and challenges in their lives, but they tend to react to it differently. When the temptation/challenge arises, they see it for the opportunity it is and use what has been given to them by God triumphing in that situation, and rejoicing in victory.

CHAPTER 7

Honeybee or Holy Bee?

The Seeking One

While "Aimless Andy" continues his self seeking journey, never becoming satisfied with his life, "Ambitious Annie" digs right in being a "happy hummer" in whatever job she fines herself doing, working for the queen and "hivedom." "Zippity do dah, zippity a, buzz a buzz buzz..."

The Seeking One (Sanctified Christian) is a far cry from the unkempt, flabby, unclean drone "Christian." The clean (holy), trim, athletically built house bee (believer) is the one who has been fed and nurtured with the teaching suitable to her development in the kingdom. She has received a portion of royal jelly (Holy Spirit) who then comes along side to help teach her what to do next in her walk with the Lord. She instinctively begins working to help keep the hive growing and safe from unwanted attacks. When the right time comes she will step out into another ministry, that of foraging, searching to find the source (The Word of God) and through an in-depth study of the Word will pass on the wisdom, knowledge and truth of God's Word to not only sustain the "tribe" but continue the growth of the "hivedom." Her work will not be in vein even if she is not physically there, because whatever she did for the "hivedom" lives on. She left a legacy. We too can leave a legacy, *"but lay up for yourselves treasures in heaven, where neither moth nor **rust** destroys and where thieves do not break in and steal."* (Matthew 6:20 NKJ)

This astonishing worker bee is the type of a true believer who is dedicated to God and willing to become a slave/servant of Christ's serving the King of Kings and His Kingdom. *"...just so he who was free when he was called is a bondservant of Christ the Messiah."* (1 Corinthians 7:22 AMP)

Remember while the worker bee is developing she is being fed with balanced food (teaching) and she starts out life from a fertilized* egg. *"And the one on whom seed was sown on the good (*fertile) soil, this is the man who hears the word and under-stands it; who indeed bears fruit and brings forth, some a hundredfold, some sixty, and some thirty."* (Matthew 13:23 NASB)

"For he shall be as a tree planted by the waters, which spreads out her roots by the river, and will not fear when heat comes, but its leaf will be green; and will not be anxious in the year of drought, nor will cease from yielding fruit." (Jeremiah 17:8 NKJ)

So much of the world is basically the reverse of the spiritual, so it is with the honeybee's life. The older she gets the harder she works. No retirement for her but continually working in the service of the Queen. She continues to have her weapon of warfare "the sword of the spirit" until the very end (no pun intended). *"Yet you do not know what your life will be like tomorrow. You are just a vapor that appears for a little while and then vanishes away."* (James 4:14 NASB)

OH! One last very important thing! The bumblebee is also called a humble bee. Maybe we should have an alternative name for the Honeybee – like Holy bee! I think we should take a vote! Okay the "Yea's" have it.

CHAPTER 8

Cottage Industries

Their very own Bee Brand.

Silk

Wrapped in silk during the most stressful time.

After the larva is sealed in its wax cell (crib), the "toddler" spins a <u>silk</u> cocoon (blanket) for itself. When it later emerges as an adult bee, <u>it can never again make silk</u>. That ability was only there while it was needed. Isn't that how it is supposed to be with the manifestation gifts of the Holy Spirit? The Holy Spirit imparts unto you whichever gift is needed at that time, so it is only there while it is needed. (Read, 1 Corinthians 12:4-11)

Wax

It takes 6 – 10 lbs. of honey to produce 1 lb. of wax.

On the abdomen of each female bee, there are four petite pockets; this is where the wax is created, and not just any kind of wax. When the bees decide to start making wax, they get hot! First, a cluster of young female bees gather together in a large pendant mass, with their wings buzzing rapidly. They hang vertically from one another, which stretches their little bodies. (Doing their warm-up stretches? "1234, 2234, 3234!") After 24 hours, each bee begins sweating wax! (Now that's what I call a work out, I'd start sweating wax too!) This white substance is called wax scales, and each bee removes it with a pair of pincers, her handy dandy tool, found on one knee joint on each side of its body. (Ha ha! Is there such a thing as bee's knees? For you younger people, back in the 1920's there was a very popular saying, "it's the bee's knees.") Actually, the bee does have leg joints but no kneecap; therefore, some feel they do not have knees as we think of knees.

Soon, wax scales litter the floor below the hanging mass of elongated bees, and other "Rosie the Riveter" bees regard it as loads of stacked steel. The "construction workers" pick it up and start building the honeycomb of hexagon shaped cells. Of course, these "gals" would be color coordinated in their tiny daffodil florescent hard hats, and with a set of handy dandy tools in her fanny pack. Each "she" bee generally makes eight (8) flakes of wax at a time. These scales are then chewed in their jaws until it becomes a soft paste that can be easily molded into six-sided cells on the honey-comb. Doesn't that sound like Bazooka bubblegum, having to get it all softened up before you can blow bubbles?

Expert chemists have never been able to match this quality of beeswax! Don't you just love it? This exceptional wax contains a variety of substances, and has a melting point of 140° F., that is higher than that of any other wax known in the world. This enables the beehive to withstand a lot of heat without it softening, and flowing, thus ruining the cells.

Bees also make a second type of wax using a different chemical formula. (Must be mother's secret recipe handed down from generation to generation.) This very specialized wax is used to seal over the top of cells in which the queen has placed eggs. Why is a special "cap wax" needed? This cap wax permits air to pass through so the larva will not suffocate. Now how ingenious is that!

Perfume
What's that fruity smell?

These miniature chemists can mix-up at least 31 different pheromones from glands in their bodies. This is besides the queen's exclusive brand. (Pepe LePew would be so proud.)

When the queen's hive is in a dilemma, she will give off a "danger scent" that alerts the other bees to the crisis. The perfume secreted by a worker bee signals other bees to draw closer and then the "alarm" is broadcast throughout the colony. This "cologne" causes the bees to cluster when swarming and it is also used when workers rediscover other bees, a queen, or the hives entrance after a period of confusion. (She must have had a little too much nectar.) Distressed and injured bees secrete a volatile material known as isopentyle acetate that smells like banana oil. "Day O, Daaaay O, daylight come and me wanta go home…." It alerts the bees to prepare them to defend the home front by surrounding and stinging the cause of the uproar. They become one fuzzy black and yellow ball of terror. ("All legs on deck, all legs on deck – Bees to your battle stations!")

Bees Bread
Yummm, warm homemade bread

Beebread is a highly nutritious food, made with 6 – 28% protein from the pollen and typically contains the 10 amino acids vital for bees. It also contains 12% honey. As the bees collect the pollen, they add an emission from special glands to it even while they are out in the field, (time management at it's best.) They also add microorganisms, which produce enzymes that release a number of chief nutrients from the pollen. While other microbes are being added to manufacture antibiotics and fatty acids in order to avoid spoilage, unnecessary microbes are being removed. In addition "Betsy Baker" adds a dash more of honey here and a pinch of nectar there until it is just the right consistency. Because of its "bready" taste it was called Beebread. (I just wonder who got that fun job of taste testing?)

Royal Jelly
Clover, Apple, or Pear?

The recently born worker, upon emerging from her cell, must eat beebread so her glands will be able to produce a unique substance for queen and country. This essence is referred to as "royal jelly" or "brood food." The jelly is a soft creamy substance that contains mandible gland secretions, 34% honey and is rich in vitamins and proteins. The distinctive jelly is manufactured in ductless glands situated in the heads of these young "nannies."

An infant "destined-for-royalty" bee is fed exclusively royal jelly, literally immersed in it (baptized?) for five days. In all other cases, royal jelly is fed to the "babes" for only the first 48 hours, and then they eat beebread for an additional three days. Just as the Holy Spirit is given to all new believers upon salvation, we all get a portion of the same Holy Spirit.

Glue
It's a sticky situation!

Bee Glue, which the "ladies" make, is called Propolis. This glue or varnish is prepared from the resin and saps that are collected. She scrapes resin off sticky buds and twigs, and loads it into her "pollen baskets." The resin will be made into bee glue to cover tree hollows, making all surfaces flawlessly smooth and also used to seal up any cracks or crevices in the hive. It's sticky when warm and even more difficult to deal with when hard, rather reminiscent of cement.

If a mouse should invade the hive, the bees sting it to death. They literally give their lives to protect their haven from the enemy. But they do not drag him out of the hive for he is excessively heavy, consequently the "undertaker bees" coat him with bee glue, which forms an airtight sarcophagus about him subsequently no odor or contamination will escape into the hive from his decomposing body.

CHAPTER 9

Wisdom & Truth

"Sweet as honey from the honeycomb"

It takes nectar and pollen in order to produce the "Bee Brand" items we just got through talking about. But for a more comprehensive depiction of the honeybees work at the flower and in the hive we need to appreciate what she does with the staples of nectar and pollen she gathers.

As she ventures from bloom to bloom, the bee cross-pollinates the flowers, a regular little horticulturist. She intuitively knows that, at any given time, she must only go to blooms of identical species. If this pollination were not completed correctly there wouldn't be any future nectar or pollen to harvest. Bees and blossoms have an affinity for each other, they must have been brought into existence at basically the same time, as they <u>cannot</u> live without each another. Wherever flowers grow, there are bees.

The "America's special flight and hover" bee has three places for storing her cargo. One is the honey tank inside her body, which she fills by sucking up syrupy nectar from the inside of the flower, through a long tube-like tongue called a Proboscis. And the other two locales are "pollen baskets" on her hind legs for carrying pollen or resin.

While inside the blossom to collect nectar she frolics around tumbling like a child playing in the surf. The splashing throws pollen grains all over her body, where they stick to feathered hairs, it's like being an electromagnet! What a major case of static cling. If she were only gathering pollen, she would pick up the yellow particles of pollen by brushing past the pollen boxes that are more often than not arranged out in front of the flower on long, thin stems, but this lady knows how to make the most of her time.

After she has filled up her "honey tank" with fluid nectar, which can take about a minute to accomplish, she will groom herself to collect the pollen clinging to the hairs on her legs and body. Most of this, she will transfer to her "pollen baskets." These baskets are a composite of a peculiar arrangement of hairs surrounding a depression on the outer surface of the hind legs. This technique will take up to three minutes to complete. I guess if women started collecting pollen they wouldn't have to shave their legs. But they sure would look strange with those enormous yellow calves!

The bee carries around with her several tools, which are an assortment of picks and combs. Talk about a woman never leaving home without her purse.

- On the middle pair of legs at the knee is a short, projecting spur, used to pack pollen into the "pollen hampers."
- On the inner part of the hind leg are a series of side combs used to scrape the body hairs of the bee.

In the process of gathering pollen, the bee moistens the pollen using a reverse gulp from her "honey tank," in order to keep it from blowing away or falling out in mid-air.

It's essential that the pollen is distributed and stored evenly between the two baskets to be aerodynamically correct. They do all this while hovering in mid-air or swinging below the flower while hanging on by one claw.

Long hairs on the front pair of legs remove pollen from her mouth and head. The middle pair of legs scrapes pollen off the thorax and front legs. The stiff comb hairs (the rake) on their rear legs comb the abdomen and take the accumulated pollen off the middle legs and push it into her "saddlebags." And finally, the spurs go to work pulling the pollen into a press made by the knee joint. When the bee bends its knee, the jaws of the press opens; when it straightens its leg, then the jaws close and the pollen is pressed down into the "pollen pouches" (that shallow trough in the middle of the hind leg.) To hold the load securely there are many curved hairs around the edge of the indentation and also a single rigid hair in the center of the basket that makes it possible to secure twice the normal amount, much like farmers use in their haystacks.

Even the bee's eyes collect pollen as hairs grow out of their eyeballs. The bee has a specially designed soft "mascara" brush to remove that particular pollen.

Wisdom – Nectar

Webster's Dictionary states: "Wisdom is knowledge that is obtained and the ability to discern inner qualities and relationships: having a wise attitude or course of action, good sense or insight."

I thought it fascinating that in scripture, knowledge and/or understanding are referred to repeatedly right along with wisdom.

Just as the bee receives two things from her source (the blossom), nectar and pollen, we receive from our source (The Word of God), wisdom and truth.

They go to their source expecting to find what the trajectory of the sun (Son) has pointed to (the answer to every need they have) and we need to go to The Word of God expecting to find wisdom and truth, just as we have received the correct directions and instructions to get us there.

Don't just read over the words or fly right by but become engaged, start rolling in and lapping up the sweet Word, storing it in your heart (our special holding chamber to store wisdom). *"Thy Word have I hid in my heart that I might not sin against Thee."* (Psalms 119:11 NASB)

Truth – Pollen

As nectar is a symbol of wisdom, pollen is a symbol of truth; what is truth? It's pure FACT. It's the Word of God made flesh. *"I am the Way, the Truth, and the Life."* (John 14:6 NKJ) Truth is the good news (Gospel) that is revealed to all that salvation has come and Jesus Christ fulfilled the Old Covenant (Testament).

As bees must have pollen so we must have truth to sustain us. Truth is the essential building blocks of our faith. *"And you shall know the truth, and the truth shall make you free."* (John 8:32 NKJ)

The Word contains everything we need to understand about salvation but we must have both wisdom and truth to complete us spiritually, like the bees have to have pollen mixed with nectar/honey in order for them to supply the hive with building materials and specialty foods. If they don't have pollen then there would be no royal jelly (Holy Spirit) given. In order to be endued with power there has to be "the power" in the first place.

Like the beebread, which is a mixture of truth and wisdom (pollen and nectar), we also need to be balanced in our faith walk. It is so important that we don't go around unbalanced in teachings, whether we are giving out misinformation in teaching or listening to it. Remember, the bee is very sure to have her pollen cargo evenly balanced; if not, she will crash and burn, not only will all her cargo be lost but she stands in jeopardy of also losing her life.

If you're unbalanced you will have a hard time standing. There is an old saying I like, "If you don't stand for something you will fall for anything." That is precisely why it is imperative that you know what you believe and why you believe it. So you can't be blown around by every wind of doctrine. *"But even if we or an angel from heaven should preach any other gospel to you than what we preached to you, let him be accursed!"* (Galatians 1:8 NKJ)

Faith - Honey
"I've got a rumbly in my tumbly!"
Winnie the Pooh

These "gals" have two stomachs one of which is entirely separate from their own food-digesting stomach. This special storage unit is referred to as a honey stomach, sac, tank, tummy, bucket, etc., although we know it is actually nectar that is stored in it at this stage of the game.

While the nectar is in her "honey" tank, various chemicals are added to it, which are secreted from glands in her head, as the bee flies around. Arriving back to the hive, the bee transfers the nectar mixture from her tongue to the tongue of another bee in the hive that then deposits the sweet concoction into six-sided storage cells. With fanning of their wings the water is evaporated to less than 18% changing the nectar solution into honey, and then wax caps are put on the honey-filled cells. (Reminds me of watching my mother make jam and pouring on the wax to seal the jar.)

Like nectar, wisdom can also be enhanced through acquired knowledge (chemicals added while in transit), life experiences/education (wing fanning to evaporate water), and maturing in the faith (storage in the cell) etc. That pretty much equals the process nectar takes to become the honey that is so desirable. A true material that is not watered down becomes extremely powerful, as you are able to give forth this knowledge with true understanding from your heart as you have experienced it yourself. This becomes the sweet truths of God (Faith.) *"So then faith comes by hearing, and hearing by the word of God."* (Romans 10:17 NKJ)

It's imperative that we feast on the Word, until it becomes alive in us where we increase in under-standing as we add a little head knowledge (glands in their heads that secrete special substances) and life experiences (those nutrients added from their bodies while flying around in their everyday life). We are to read, rehash and research with other infor-mation, i.e. Hebraic teaching, commentaries, Bible maps, dictionaries, and scripture previously known, thereby, increasing our knowledge and wisdom to be able to distribute to others. *"The mouth of the righ-teous utters wisdom, and his tongue speaks justice."* (Psalm 37:30 NASB) This holds with our pattern that nectar is the Wisdom of God. *"This book of the law shall not depart from your mouth, but you shall medi-tate on it day and night, so that you may be careful to do according to all that is written in it; for then you will make your way prosperous, and then you will have success."* (Joshua 1:8 AMP)

Honey is the real sweet truths of God or a faith that has become so delicious, because you own it, its part of you – your experience makes it real. You know that you know that you know! You will not be shaken from the Truth. You have become settled in your faith and standing on a firm foundation.

We, as followers of Christ, need to emulate the honeybee by seeking out the Word of God, searching out the basic truths and/or promises in God's Word through study and prayer. *"Study and be eager and do your utmost to present yourself to God approved (tested by trial), a workman who has no cause to be ashamed, correctly analyzing and accurately dividing [rightly handling and skillfully teaching] the Word of Truth."* (2 Tim 2:15 NASB) Faith becomes the "honey" to us as this truth becomes endued with power, as we believe. His knowledge with our understanding is the sweetness of having the ability to relate this knowledge to others.

"Pleasant words are like a honeycomb, sweetness to the soul and health to the bones." (Proverbs 16:24 NKJ) Not only do we use these truths and promises to nourish ourselves with spiritual food but also to feed others who are still maturing in their walk in the Lord (which includes us all). We never stop advancing onward and upward - *"Brethren, I do not regard myself as having laid hold of it yet; but one thing I do: forgetting what lies behind and reaching forward to what lies ahead, I press on toward the*

goal for the prize of the upward call of God in Christ Jesus." (Philippians 3:13-14 NASB)

CHAPTER 10

Dance Repertoire

Macarena or Hoochy Choochy?

Think of the worker bee as a woman on a mission. When she strikes it rich, she fills her tummy, packs her "bags" and returns with the news to her own hive, "Hallelujah! The source has been found."

The waiting bees are so anxious they will often crowd the returning "bearer of Good News"; so that the closest bees to the "missionary" are instinctively deputized for crowd control, and they have to push the others back to give her legroom to boogie! Yep, she is so excited with what she has to tell them she can't stand still. She's a dancin' machine.

Honeybees communicate with one another not only phonetically and kinetically but also by using distinctive chemicals, and odors to broadcast important messages and warnings of danger. There is a miniature, scent organ at the top of each antenna. (Can't get much smaller as we are already talking of miniscule portions as it is.) Scientists have discovered the bee has 170 odor receptors so they can distinguish between a gazillion different flowering species using these olfactory clues, much like the hairs in our nose. Tonal qualities of sounds produced by bees suggest that as many as 14 moods can be communicated. The gyrating audiences of bees decode and personally practice the trip in miniature "dance rehearsal" before leaving on their own nectar and pollen trek.

There has been considerable amount of controversy in regards to how a bee transmits her essential information to the other bees inside a dark hive. It wasn't until the 1990's that the full sensory of their dance language was discovered. Up until that time bees were thought to be deaf, but possibly could feel vibrations. Through labor-intensive study most of the controversy has now been cleared up.

When putting together all the pieces of these various studies we are now able to reveal how the dance language works. This dance language is clearly an incredibly complicated, and a vastly advanced system.

Climbing onto the vertical honeycomb, usually close to the entrance, she performs one of the two dances in her repertoire. If the nectar source is less than 30 feet from the hive she will do the "Round" dance. (Not the square dance as there are no partners to "do-si-do" with, she's a one-woman show.) She does this by running in narrow circles, and then suddenly reversing direction to her original course. She may repeat the dance several times at the same location or move to another stage and do an encore performance. After the round dance has ended, she often distributes food to the bees following her, being quite the little hostess at intermission. The pattern of the dance communicates that the source is close to the hive, but she gives no directions. The bees will instinctively know to circle the hive in ever widening circles to find the source of her quest.

If the cache is a long way off, and especially if it's only one tree or small patch of flowers, then the dance is different. The information must be particularly detailed and cautiously given since the bees might get lost searching for what they cannot live without. This truly can be a life or death situation, a real Indian Jones adventure.

The second dance number is the "Waggle" dance. She will do the "Hustle" along a straight line, vigorously wagging her posterior as she goes. A true belly dancer and we thought people came up with that! At the same time, the bee emits a train of buzzing sounds at a low frequency with pulse duration of about 20 milliseconds and a repetition frequency of 30 seconds. The hum is produced by the wing beats. Wow! Humming and dancing at the same time, a real Ginger Rogers or Hannah Montana!

The onlookers receive these signals through their "ears" located in their antennae, which are always held out towards the artiste. Because these organs are bilateral – one on the left and one the right – the bees "watching" the performance can use them to moderate their position in respect to the "ballerina" and therefore comprehend the direction to the food. At the same time, the "dance students" can make her pause and give them a taste of the nectar by using a squeaking sound that vibrates the honeycomb. These appetizers give her audience additional hints about the taste and aroma of the food source. The bees attend the dancing exhibition for a while and then fly out to find the source on their own.

Each dance can be made different by changing the "tempo" duration of buzzing sounds and the length of the straight run portion of the dance, measured in seconds. As the distance to the food source increases, the duration of the waggling segment of the dance also increases. It is only during the waggle portion of the dance that the sounds are produced. At the end of the straight line, (It's the original line dance!) she turns left and walks in a partial circle back to the starting point.

During this part of the performance the bees will use their antennae to whiff the aroma that has been left on her by whatever the dancer found. She then runs straight down the runway again along that same line, circling right this time back to the starting point where she does an encore routine. I wonder how many curtain calls are normal?

The "Waggle" dance communication forms a figure 8, and it's <u>at the cross</u> points of the 8 that gives the trajectory of the nectar in relation to the sun (<u>Son</u>). As the bee dances on the wall of the honeycomb, the position of the sun is always down. If the bee moves up the comb wall at 19° to the left of vertical that means the source of nectar will be located 19° to the left of the sun.

The speed in which she circles reveals the distance. The farther the flowers are the slower she circles back.

If she does 10 laps in 15 seconds, the "stockpile" is 300 feet away but if two revolutions in 15 seconds are done, then the goodies are four miles away. The length of her "hippy hippy shake" tells the quantity available at that specific location. The more vigorously she shakes the more abundant the supply.

The round weaving dance indicates nearby nectar and/or pollen and a tail-wagging figure-eight dance indicates distant nectar and/or pollen. It continues to amaze me that **this is all done in the darkness of the hive with no ordinary light**, or even ultraviolet light, as they are not able to sense the infrared light from the moving of the bee's body that is dancing before them. They must be excellent at Blind Man's Bluff. Just a side note, darkness is not always a bad thing. It was in the darkness of the cloud that covered Mt. Sinai that Moses met with God.

Before the forager bees depart they must fill their specially designed honey stomachs with just the right amount of fuel – not too much or too little. No need for extra weight but enough fuel to get them back to their happy home. The honey "fuel" is so powerful that a pinhead-sized speck will whirl the bee's powerful yet delicate wings for about a quarter of a mile. A foraging bee gets about seven million flight miles to one gallon of honey. (WOW! Pretty expensive when you know what it costs the bee to make it.) In her whole life she will only produce about 1/10th of a pound of honey.

There is still much to learn such as what purpose the bees possess with the ability to distinguish between different pitched sounds. In addition, perhaps they use similar airborne sounds in ways that we do not even suspect at this time. In the hopes of revealing their communication system in full, the researchers will continue to eavesdrop on their conversations.

I love how those "little girl scouts" come back and teach others through their "Pentecostal Jive" where and how to find "The Source."

It's through others hearing and following the example given (being imitators of Christ) that gets us all excited so we want to venture out and rally round to build the Kingdom.

We need to remember that as we go to our source (The Word of God), we need to make sure we have a relationship with the Father. Have you been "dancing" (communicating) with the Lord? Is your mind cleansed and spiritually fit to be able to obtain the wisdom and truth you seek?

During the dance demo the bee tells the others not only the direction to the source but gives a tempting taste - *"Taste and see that the LORD is good."* (Psalm 34:8 NASB) - so they too can find the source, taste the goodness, gather nectar and bring it back to the hive where it is made into honey (believer's faith.)

Another form of communication the bee uses is fragrance and every species has a different fragrance.

We too have fragrances. You can't help but exchange your aroma with others who are in close proximity to you. Believes who are surrounded with other believers in corporate, intercessory, and warfare prayer will have those fragrances mingling around them as the prayers ascend on high. But let's say you are in a crowd of smokers and even though you are not smoking you will come away smelling of that relational experience. Selah (in some translations this word in found in the Psalms, it is an instructional word meaning – Pause and think about it.)

> *"And walk in love, as Christ also has loved us and given Himself for us, as an offering and a sacrifice to God for a <u>sweet-smelling aroma</u>."* (Ephesians 5:22 NKJ) *"and when He had taken the scroll, the four living creatures and the twenty-four elders prostrated themselves before the Lamb. Each was holding a harp (lute or guitar), and they had golden bowls full of incense (fragrant spices and gums for burning), <u>which are the prayers of God's people</u> (the Saints)."* (Revelation 5:8 AMP)

A fully loaded honeybee will fly home at 15 miles an hour; she literally makes a "bee line" straight back to the hive veering only for obstacles in her path. If you happen to be a new unexpected obstacle you may get stung! So take the advise of (Proverbs 4:26-27 AMP) *"Consider well the path of your feet, and let all your ways be established and ordered aright. Turn not aside to the right hand or to the left; remove your foot from evil."*

CHAPTER 11

Five, the Number of Grace
Sight, Smell, Hearing, Taste & Touch

In Scripture, numbers can have a significant meaning, as every letter in the Hebrew alphabet has a numeric value. Here are just a few:

One - Beginning,
Two - Witness or division,
Three - Godhead, Divine completeness,
Four - Earth, creation,
Five - Grace,
Six - Man,
Seven - Perfection,
Eight - New Beginnings.

As five is the number of grace I can see where the honeybee's five senses of sight, smell, hearing, taste and touch fit the scenario nicely.

Seeing Red?

The honeybee has five eyes; two are large compound eyes that detect shape and color. The remaining three are called simple eyes that are positioned in a triangle formation between the two compound eyes on top of their forehead. These three are only used to detect light and dark. (Good & Evil?) The bee can distinguish the colors blue, yellow and ultraviolet (which we can not see) but they are insensitive to the color red and infrared.

Bees are guided by "the polarity of light." They operate something like a compass. Waves of light travel directly outward from the sun in all directions. The tiny angle of each shaft of sunlight (sunbeam) is analyzed by the eye and brain of the bee, telling the directional information in their relation to the sun and location of the hive. They can even sense the slant of UV light on cloudy days.

As a true believer, we don't need to see the Blood of Christ as (John 20: 29 NASB) states that *"blessed are those that don't see and believe anyway."* It's God who allows us into His presence because of the "red" Blood of Christ, which covers us and makes us able to stand clean before our Father. He needs to see the "red" Blood of Christ not us!

Dragon's Breath
Where's My Mints?

The bee's mouthparts consist of a straw-like tube that "Sucking Suzy" uses to feed on liquid food, either the nectar of flowers or the honey stored within the hive.

Oh that our tongues were only adapted to that of sharing the Wisdom and Word of God! Proverbs 18:21 (NASB) states, *"death and life are in the power of the tongue, and those who love it will eat its fruit."* The bee also holds life and death in her tongue, for if they do not collect the nectar, the entire hive would die. And so it is with the Believer, if we stop feasting on the Word of God we will die spiritually.

When you use your tongue, do you become a fire-breathing dragon? Do you need to use those heavenly breath freshener's (prayers/praises – sweet smelling savor) to keep that dragon's breath under control?

We need to strive to be like the honeybee. Their straw-like tongue structure is used for only three (3) purposes: collecting, transporting the precious nectar and feeding themselves.

Do you ever wonder why you find yourself becoming complacent in your spiritual life and not feeling any desire to read scripture or pray? It's because you have stopped feeding your spirit and it is withering away. "They" say that if you don't eat for three or four days then you loose the desire and/or the cravings especially for sugar and carbohydrates. You don't have to worry about calories, so eat up! Pig Out! Have a spectacular feast with the Lord every day. I promise you, your spirit won't get obese and unhealthy, as we are to also exercise our faith, run that race and fight the good fight etc. Get out there and "play flight", exercise your spiritual faculties as you do your physical.

It is of the utmost importance that our tongues be kept under guard. *"He who guards his mouth and his tongue, guards his soul from troubles...* (Proverbs 21:23 NASB) *keep your tongue from evil and your lips from speaking deceit."* (Peter 3:10 & Psalm 34:13 NASB)

The bee's taste receptors distinguish the same tastes we do. However, the bee's threshold to sour and salty is lower than ours while its threshold to bitter and sweet is off the charts. The relatively high threshold to sweet gives them an extremely efficient ability to find the superior nectar with the least amount of water; thus, expending less energy for a better product of honey. The very sweetness of God's Word and wisdom is like honeycomb, *"more to be desired are they than gold, yea, than much fine gold; sweeter also than honey and the droppings of the honeycomb."* (Psalm 19:10 NASB)

We need the ability to detect watered down and unbalanced doctrine and teachings.

Those Who Have Ears to Hear...

These "happy hummers" have two slender exquisitely formed antennae, attached at the top front portion of their heads, which are multi-functional for communication. Each antenna consists of 11 – 12 segments each performing a task such as smelling, hearing, tasting and touch. The 2nd joint has been discovered to be what we would refer to as an "ear."

Until recently bees were unknown to have the equivalent of ears. But the Lord said that He whistled for them and so they must have had ears to hear Him. Of course, God was right all along. If the honeybee were to be a pattern of the ultimate church, they would have to be able to hear, as we are told that we must know the voice of the shepherd. *"To him the doorkeeper opens, and the sheep hear His voice, and He calls his own sheep by name and leads them out."* (John 10:3 NASB)

And don't forget the trumpet blast! *"In a moment, in the twinkling of an eye, at the last trumpet. For the trumpet will sound, and the dead will be raised incorruptible, and we shall be changed!"* (1Corinthians 15:52 NKJ) We too will be flying in our own nuptial flight (the Rapture) to arrive at the Marriage Supper of the Lamb.

The antennae must be frequently cleaned as resin and other substances coat them while they are gathering their resources. On the front legs is a movable piece of tough tissue, which can be raised like a lid making an opening. On the edge of this opening are short stiff hairs. The "little lady" bends an antenna toward the left and opens the leg gate, drops in the antenna, closes the gate and then draws the antenna back and forth between the stiff hairs and presto change-o its clean. (Sort of like using her antennae as floss.)

Similar to their antennae, we have to keep our spiritual censors clean, always ready and alert to every situation.

How do we keep our spiritual antennae clean? By washing of course! *"So that He might sanctify her, having cleansed her by the washing of water with the Word."* (Ephesians 5:26 NASB) *"Not by works of righteousness which we have done, but according to His mercy He saved us, through the washing of regeneration and renewing of the Holy Spirit."* (Titus 3:5 NKJ) If our spiritual antennae are covered in garbage, we will not be able to smell the fragrance of the Source or hear the trumpet sound or the battle cry. We need to be on guard at all times to the enemy's attack and/or the Lord's Return!

CHAPTER 12

Weapons of Warfare

What's my mouth got to do with it?

These "busy buzzers" have surprisingly powerful jaws. The Holy Scripture tells us that Samson used the jawbone of an ass to kill a thousand men. Now the bee's jawbone is slightly smaller but still powerful enough in their "Lilliputian" world to be used as a valuable weapon also. Under normal circumstances her mandibles (jaws) maneuver solids such as pollen, wax, and debris in the hive.

They chew the wax scales, making the wax palpable for use in creating the physical structure of the honeycomb. Could that be where we use our mouths/jaws in teaching and making The Word clear and understandable to any age believer in the body?

I think of the cow in how it masticates its food, rehashing, and/or chewing its cud over and over until she has thoroughly prepared it for proper digestion so her body gets every single nutrient out of the food to sustain her. How, like David, meditating on The Word day and night. *"I will remember my song in the night; I will meditate with my heart, and my spirit ponders..."* (Psalm 77:6 NASB) *"I will meditate on all your work and muse on your deeds..."* (Psalm 77:12 NASB) *"I will meditate on your precepts and regard your ways..."* (Psalm 119:15 NASB) *"And I shall lift up my hands to your commandments, which I love; and I will meditate on your statutes."* (Psalm 119:48 NASB)

The honeybee's jaw is also used for pinching and biting. Remember how they chase the queen around so she is physically fit to fly? Well, we also need to be in spiritual shape and ready to go on our flight [the Rapture] when He calls for His Bride. The Bible states He is coming for a bride without spot or wrinkle! *"That He might present the church to Himself in glorious splendor, without spot or wrinkle or any such things [that she might be holy and fault-less.]"* (Ephesians 5:27 NASB)

You know that it's going to take some exhortation and heavy encouragement in love to get some of us to the place where we are capable of flight! And what it takes to get us there isn't always pleasant. (Ouch! That smarts!!) But we have to get rid of all that excess baggage we keep carrying around and leave it at the cross, where the Lord takes care of it. *"In a moment, in the twinkling of an eye, at the last trumpet; for the trumpet will sound, and the dead will be raised imperishable, and we will be changed."* (1 Corinthians 15:51-53 NASB)

Those jaws sound like weapons of warfare to me. How many times have you used your voice, and worked your jaws to proclaim The Word of God in overthrowing the adversary in some situation? We need to keep the iron hot and ready to press out those wrinkles we keep putting in our wedding dress. "Oh, I hope it fits right. Do you think I look too fat?"

Wasn't that great about the queen sounding a battle cry? We are to be doing battle – spiritual warfare – Blow the Shofar! In the Old Testament the armies would go out with priests before the army sounding a battle cry using the Word of the Lord. *"And when he had consulted with the people, He appointed those who should sing to the LORD and who should praise the beauty of holiness, as they went out before the army and were saying, 'Praise the LORD, for His mercy endures forever.'"* (2 Chronicles 20:21 NKJ)

We are also told to shout onto the Lord *"But let all those rejoice who put their trust in You; Let them ever shout for joy, because You defend them; Let those also who love Your name Be joyful in You..."* (Psalm 5:11 NKJ)

As God has given to the honeybee every instrument that she needs to complete her work, we are also given gifts and talents to do the same thing. *"So we, who are many, are one body in Christ, and individually members one of another. Since we have gifts that differ according to the grace given to us, each of us is to exercise them accordingly: if prophecy, according to the proportion of his faith; if service, in his serving; or he who teaches, in his teaching;"* (Romans 12:5-7 NASB) This verse corresponds perfectly with how the bees use different talents at different stages of their life, as the Creator has placed in their DNA.

At times warfare is done on an individual basis (using their own sword – stinger), but many times it is done in unity with other believers, which raises the heat level against the enemy. Could this be <u>fervent prayer</u>, unity of the body in prayer — exercising their faith? *"Confess your trespasses to one another, and pray for one another, that you may be healed. The effectual fervent prayer of a righteous man avails much."* (James 5:16 NKJ)

God has equipped us with every good gift to withstand the enemy and send him in full retreat! *"Therefore take up the full armor of God, so that you will be able to resist in the evil day, and, having done everything, to stand. Stand firm therefore, having girded your loins with truth, and having put on the breastplate of righteousness, and having shod your feet with the preparation of the gospel of peace; in addition to all taking up the shield of faith, with which you will be able to extinguish all the flaming arrows of the evil one. And take the helmet of salvation, and the sword of the Spirit, which is the Word of God: with all prayer and petition pray at all times in the Spirit, and with this in view, be on the alert with all perseverance and petition for all the saints,"* (Ephesians 6:13-18 NASB)

Researchers have used a MRI to scan bee brains and have found that the honeybee processes every emotion except fear! If we are wearing the full armor of God we shouldn't have to deal with fear either.

Did you happen to notice that the worker bees have weapons of warfare but the drones don't? If the drones are attacked they have no hope of survival.

CHAPTER 13

Marvelous Mysteries

Let's Fly!

Now you may have heard someone say, "Scientists don't understand how bees can fly as the bee's wings are too small for their bodies," or some such thing. I always loved that God's creation would defy the "Laws of Science," but the secret to the bee's awesome ability to fly has been figured out and it shows the Amazing Designer at His best.

The wing-beat speed fueled by the propulsion of the muscular thorax enables the precious insect to become airborne. The wings and muscles attached to them have been so impeccably calculated that in flight the wings move in a figure eight (8) design, which makes it possible for the bee to fly in <u>any</u> direction – up, down, sideways, backwards, forwards, or any combination of those directions. They can even remain motionless hovering in front of a blossom. This arrangement of muscles and wing structure is complicated in the extreme, yet the result is one of the most efficient flight systems on earth. The adult worker bee is the only flying creature capable of carrying almost 100% of her own weight. Even our heavy freight equipment can only carry about 25% of its weight.

The "fuzzy flier" has two pair of wings that work too well to have occurred by chance. The wings have to be small enough to get inside buds just opening, long skinny tube-like blossoms or the minute opening of the hive and yet large enough to carry her weight in flight. It appears that the larger front wing on each side of its body has a row of hooks on its trailing edge. These hooks attach to the rear wing when in flight, going from four small wings on the ground to two large wings when in the air. Upon landing, the two wings instinctively unhook and again overlap greatly reducing their size. Sounds like God's Velcro to me. *"...and there is nothing new under the sun."* (Ecclesiastes 1:9 NKJ)

In examining the physical body of these "magnificent flying machines," let's discover some of the astonishing hidden mysteries.

These "frequent flyers" have wings with "God's Velcro" that gives reinforcement when needed and folds neatly out of the way when in tight places, *"May He grant you out of the rich treasury of His Glory to be strengthened and **reinforced** with mighty power in the inner man by the Holy Spirit [Himself] indwelling your innermost being and personality."* (Ephesians 3:16 AMP) Oh, how cool!

The "Velcro" wings are a symbol of the Holy Spirit as referred to in John 14:26 (AMP) *"But the Comforter (Counselor, Helper, Intercessor, Advocate, Strengthener, Standby), the Holy Spirit, Whom the Father will send in My name [...to represent Me and act on My behalf], He will teach you all things. And He will cause you to recall (...bring to your remembrance) everything I have told you."* Just as the honeybee's reinforced wings give them the capability to do in the natural what seems impossible; the Holy Spirit gives us the power to do all things through Christ. Just think, one day we too will "fly" when He comes to get His Bride, and won't that befuddle the minds of unregenerate man.

When we find ourselves in tight places or feeling all alone, we need to remember that the Holy Spirit is still carefully tucked away and ready at a moments notice. He is our hero, not putting on great displays of "barn storming routines," but still attached and ready to allow us to rely on His flight power. *Then he said to me, "This is the word of the LORD to Zerubbabel saying, 'Not by might nor by power, but by My Spirit,' says the LORD of hosts."* (Zechariah 4:6 NKJ) Being able to adapt to whatever situation we find ourselves in whether sailing high in the sky or in a claustrophobic pit. Sometimes it is stepping out into the unknown by faith and feeling the Holy Spirit "like the wind beneath our wings" or handling a difficult situation (traps). There are times when we do not understand what to do or how to pray, and that is when the Holy Spirit makes intercession for us. *"Likewise the Spirit also helps our infirmities: for we know not what we should pray for as we ought: but the Spirit itself makes intercession for us with groanings which cannot be uttered."* (Romans 8:26 NKJ)

Fun Fact: Bee researcher Thomas Seeley has likened a bee flying at a speed of about 15 mph traveling 3 ½ miles in a single flight home would be equal to a person 5 feet tall "flying" 375 miles.

CHAPTER 14

The Matrix

Home Sweet Home (No pun intended!)

Webster's Dictionary states the definition of Matrix is, "Something within which something else originates or develops." I think that the honeybee colony, which consists of 10,000 to 60,000 or more single bees, certainly qualifies as a matrix. Considered individually or together, they are a masterpiece of design. Although they all come from the same queen, there are three different types of bees in the hive and each one knows exactly what their role is at each stage of life.

The hive consists of one queen, up to hundreds of drones and tens of thousands of worker bees, who total 85% of the hives population.

The house bee uses her own special blend of beeswax to shape it into a waterproof honeycomb. This pliable material is pushed in concert from all directions, forming thousands of six-sided cells on both sides of the comb. The bees crawl into the cups and press them into shape, each cell the size of an adult bee. Each hexagon shaped cell is a work of faultless craftsmanship. Would God have it any other way? The cell size varies from the smallest of 5 mm diameter for the worker bee to 7 mm diameter for the drone. Drawing long thin threads of varnish/glue through the wax reinforces it, so when the wax hardens around the threads, it's like concrete reinforced with wire. How ingenious is that. Again, God had the idea first!

The "cups" containing the eggs and developing bees are kept in the most protected area of the hive near the heart of the honeycomb, at 95° F. That area is called the "brood nest." It resembles a bull's eye configuration. Arranged around this "protected community" more "condos" are constructed for the storage of pollen. Around the pollen cells are still more "storage containers" (Tupperware at it's finest) filled with honey.

The cell walls are only 1/350th of an inch thick! This would make a sharp top cell edge, even for padded bees' feet, so the top edge is given an extra final coating of wax to thicken it, giving it a rounded edge, and increasing the thickness to 1/80th of an inch.

Only three shapes could possibly be used in building the cells: the triangle, square, or the hexagon. When testing out these three shapes, we find that the hexagon holds more honey in the same space than the other two. It also uses less wax to construct and the shared sides require even a smaller amount wax.

After Isaac Newton invented calculus, it was discovered that the shape of the cell is more marvelous then what was first thought. The cap at the top of each cell is a pyramid composed of three rhombuses. Complex mathematics reveal that this shape requires less wax than any other shape, and it enables the cells to be butted up closely against one another, with no loss of space. So what we have here is a ten-sided prism. It's The Great Mathematician at work again.

When the world looks at The Church (body of believers), they should see a beautiful, awesome structure that WOWS the natural world in its shear mathematical proportions and design – not being hindered by the laws of this world. Perfect in uniformity, expressly designed to hold an abundance of wisdom and knowledge, faith, grace and mercy that natural thinking cannot comprehend how it is possible. A formation that defies gravity, scientific laws, etc... *This is Paul speaking – "When you read this you can understand my insight into the mystery of Christ. This mystery was never disclosed to human beings in past generations as it has now been revealed to His holy apostles and prophets by the Holy Spirit... Also to enlighten all men and make plain to them what is the plan [regarding the Gentiles and providing for the salvation of all men] of the mystery kept hidden through the ages and concealed until now in [the mind of] God Who created all things by Christ Jesus. [The purpose is] that through the church the complicated, many-sided wisdom of God* **(the honeycomb!)** *in all its infinite variety and innumerable aspects* *might now be made known to the angelic rulers and authorities (principalities and powers) in the heavenly sphere.*" (Ephesians 3:4 -10 AMP) I like to think that the underlined portion of the above verse could also refer to the hidden mystery of the honeybee.

We should be an exceedingly large diverse group of individuals all working for the good of the whole, never thinking of ourselves but what is best for the whole body—who are ready to put their lives on the line—to protect "The Bride of Christ."

As the honeybee seemingly operates on auto-pilot going from one job to the next according to the seasons in her life, we are told to be content in whatever circumstance we find ourselves— no grumbling or complaining—just bloom where you are planted with each new season of your life in Christ. Make the most of the opportunity that is given to you. Look at what the Apostle Paul accomplished for the Kingdom of God while in prison, the letters to the Ephesians, Philippians, Colossians, etc. *"Not that I speak from want, for I have learned to be content in whatever circumstances I am. I know how to get along with humble means, and I also know how to live in prosperity; in any and every circumstance I have learned the secret of being filled and going hungry, both of having abundance and suffering need. I can do all things through Him who strengthens me."* (Philippians 4:11-13 NASB)

There would be no need to have constant supervision, as everyone instinctively would do what is needed at the time, automatically outfitted with the talent or ability to do the appropriate task. A perfectly tuned machine that continually regenerates and renews it self and so intricate that it is impossible to determine if one member is greater than another. (Reminds me of the Sesame Street song, "One of these things is not like the other, one of these things just doesn't belong.) Is it the bee or the egg, the nectar or pollen, the honey or beebread, or maybe even the royal jelly?

We are the Body of Christ and each part is important, whether you are the heart or the wax in the ear (nice sedge way to bees, right?) there is a place and purpose for you in the Body of Christ. *"For as we have many members in one body, but all the members do not have the same function, so we in Christ being many, are one body in Christ, and individually members of one another"*(Romans 12:4-5 NKJ)

When we look into the makeup of the "body" there is one head and we know that Christ is the head of the Church. If we were a true type of the honeybee, 85% of the body would be workers/laborers and there would be no holding back the "Great Commission." *"Go therefore and make disciples of all the nations, baptizing them in the name of the Father and of the Son and of the Holy Spirit, teaching them to observe all things that I have commanded you; and lo, I am with you always, even to the end of the age." Amen.* (Matthew 28:19-20 NKJ)

But we have it just reversed - 15% are the workers and 85% are the drones (those who say they believe, give lip service and having an appearance of godliness, but no substance etc. *Therefore the Lord said: "In as much as these people draw near*

*with their mouths and honor Me with their lips, But
have removed their hearts far from me, and their fear
toward Me is taught by the commandment of men."*
(Isaiah 29:13 NKJ)

The center of the hive where the queen and brood
nest is situated stays a constant 95° F. When the
weather drops to 57° F or less, the bees congregate
around the queen and generate extra heat by increasing
their metabolism. By breathing faster! (Revving their
engines, vroom VARHOOOM.) Other bees collect all
over the inside of the outer walls and provide "fuzzy"
insulation for the hive. If the weather remains cool,
the bees in the center rotate with the bees on the walls,
everyone equally sharing in the warmth.

When the weather becomes too warm "ventila-
tion" bees stand at the entrance rapidly fanning their
wings to aerate the honeycomb with cooler external
air. If the weather becomes still warmer, other bees fly
out of the hive and bring back water in their honey
sacks to wet the inside of the outer walls of the hive!
At that point, the fanning of the rest of the bees' wings,
and this <u>includes the drones</u>, rapidly cools the walls as
the water evaporates.

It is a very important asset to our Christian walk
to be on familiar terms with how to regulate the ther-
mostat especially when we get older. ("It must be a
hot flash!" (Right ladies?) *"So because you are luke-
warm and neither cold nor hot, I will spew you out of
my mouth"* (Revelation 3:16 NASB) You will notice
He wanted us either cold or hot, whatever was needed

to meet the situation. Like food you want the hot – hot, and the cold – cold, not room temperature.

When the hive is too warm, the bees will pump their abdominal system to move air through their spiracles, little holes in the sides of their bodies. Bee conduits! Interesting, don't you think, that they do this ventilating through the body not the mouth! And in those times when little hot spots appear, we have the capability to put out those flames peacefully. *"See how great a forest is set aflame by such a small fire!"* (James 3:5) and *"Blessed are the peacemakers."* (Matthew 5:9 NKJ) If we need to put out fires that are being set then lets get the water of the Word and our help of the Holy Spirit (wings) to take care of the problem, bear in mind, don't use Dragon's breath that will only add to the flames!

When others are cooling down, we are to help light those fires of renewal and revival. If it's heat you need, get those engines revived up – and vibrate!! How do we stir up the flames of revival? By prayer - fasting - teaching and preaching the Word, etc.

We are also to be diligent in our walk with the Lord. Just as the bees have an innate knowledge of what to do when temperatures change, we need to be standing ready also to, *"Preach the Word! Be ready in season and out of season. Convince, rebuke, and exhort, with all longsuffering and teaching."* (2 Timothy 4:2 NKJ)

The honeybee has three legs on each side of her thorax and each leg has five main joints, plus teeny segments that make up the foot. With these five joints, each appendage can twist, turn, and move in just about any direction needed. (She could put a contortionist to shame; I have trouble walking on my two legs with joints that only bend one way!) The miniscule parts of the foot and sharp tips on the claws of each foot, enables her to walk on any rough surface. Between its claws a cushioned pad allows her to walk on smooth and/or slippery surfaces. I've heard it said, "If your foot slips, you may recover your balance; but if your tongue slips, you cannot recall your words." No matter what type of surface we find ourselves on God will give us the ability to walk on it.

The Most Fascinating Fact of All

All this knowledge and equipment comes from the DNA code placed by the queen and drone in her eggs. Yet she is not passing on information that she does, for she never goes out and gathers any nectar or pollen, nor does she make any beebread, wax, or cells. Not once does she ever dance the "honey dance" or even bother to watch it being done. Yet she is the one that passes along all the coding for all the parts, processes, and accomplishments of all the bees in the hive, astonishing! The more that is revealed of God's creation the more complex it becomes, and they say it just evolved.

There are still a lot of controversial ideas being studied while trying to understand the honeybee better, demonstrating that we still have not discovered all the mysteries of the bee.

Just how smart are the honeybee's?

"Researchers at Princeton University thought they might be able to outsmart the bees. After the bees learned where their food source was, the scientists moved it 50 meters (164 feet) farther away from the hive. They were surprised to find that it took the bees less than one minute to find the moved food. So they moved it again, the second time precisely 50 meters (164 feet) farther away. It still took the bees less than a minute to locate it!

But then the <u>scientists discovered the bees were smarter than they were</u>. When the researchers moved the honey source a third time, —the bees were waiting at the exact location it was to be moved to—<u>before the researchers arrived with the food</u>!"

CHAPTER 15

Type/Shadow or Symbol Challenge

In the below list of numbers **1 – 8**, see if you can find the matching type/shadow or symbol in the list of **A – H.**

The Honeybee 1 - 8

1. Source (Flowers)
2. Nectar
3. Pollen
4. Honey
5. Beebread
6. Royal Jelly
7. Worker bee
8. Drone

The Type/Shadow/Symbol A - H

A. Wisdom
B. "Christian"

C. Truth
D. Equips the Saints
E. Sanctified Christian
F. Word of God
G. Powerful Knowledge & Understanding
    (Faith)
H. Holy Spirit

For answers see last page of this chapter.

Other Points to Ponder

Could the Queen be another symbol of the Holy Spirit? She is consistently supplying the eggs "the newborn" and (1 Corinthians 12:3 AMP) states *"And no one can [really] say, Jesus is [my] Lord, except by and under the power and influence of the Holy Spirit."*

The Holy Spirit is usually looked upon as having the feminine attributes of the God Head – El Shaddai "The many breasted one, the one who nourishes." The queen also eats nothing but the "royal jelly" her whole existence. So I will put this out there for you to think on. Could the queen bee represent the Holy Spirit? Totally filled with nothing but royal jelly, it is through her that the babes in Christ are birthed. Without her there would be no converts. Cool huh!

Now I can't write a book about the honeybee without having to give my opinion on something I ran across while doing the research for this book.

I've heard honey referred to in a most unpleasant term of bee vomit.

Webster's Dictionary states: Vomit: an act or instance of disgorging the contents of the stomach through the mouth, eject violently or abundantly, akin to nausea.

This definitely does not represent what happens in the transferring of the nectar from one bee's specially designed holding area (stomach) to another specially prepared chamber (stomach). This process is accomplished by passing the nectar from their tube-like tongue to tube-like tongue, not out the mouth violently! It is also done voluntarily and is a natural and normal process with no involuntary spasmodic movements.

So my answer would be NO! It is not bee vomit. Honey is one of the purest foods on earth.

More Facts You Might Be Interested in Knowing.

Fact: Since all the sperm cells produced by a drone are genetically identical, bee sisters are more closely related than full sisters of other animals where the sperm is not genetically identical.

Fact: Recent research (1998) seems to indicate that bees do sleep, as they remain motionless for long periods of time and need more stimuli to "wake" them up. (Well the poor things are probably exhausted and have sleep depravation!)

Fact: In order to make a pound of honey, a bee living close to clover fields would have to travel

13,000 miles, or about 4 times the distance from New York City to San Francisco!

Fact: White or light colors are associated with flowers and are non-threatening that's why beekeepers wear light or white clothes.

Fact: When the surrounding and stinging technique is used to kill a queen perceived as intruding or defective, it's called "balling the queen." (Makes me think of a Royal Ball.)

Fact: A typical colony may use up to 100 lbs. of pollen for brood rearing each year.

Types/Shadows/Symbols Challenge – Answers*
*at least to my way of thinking.

1. *Source* **(F) Word of God**
2. *Nectar* **(A) Wisdom**
3. *Pollen* **(C) Truth**
4. *Honey* **(G) Powerful Knowledge & Understanding (Faith)**
5. *Beebread* **(D) Equips the Saints**
6. *Royal Jelly* **(H) Holy Spirit**
7. *Worker bee* **(E) Sanctified Christian**
8. *Drone* **(B) "Christian"**

CHAPTER 16

Disappearing Act?
It just fits

While working on this book my husband, Ken, and I started hearing news reports of honey-bees mysteriously disappearing, not even finding the bodies.

"Stefan Lovgren in Los Angeles for <u>National Geographic News</u>
February 23, 2007

Without a trace, something is causing bees to vanish by the thousands. Researchers are closely watching what is happening to bee colonies currently pollinating California's 1.4-billion-dollar almond crop. Almonds are 100 percent dependent on bee pollination.

Hackenberg said. 'There were no dead bees, no bees on the ground, just empty boxes. In almost 50 years as a beekeeper, I've never seen anything like it.'"

I had to chuckle to myself when my husband asked me what I thought about this in relation to the types/shadows of my book. I quipped, "what a great ending to my book. It's just another type/shadow of the bee – The Rapture!"

Albert Einstein once said, "If the bee disappeared off the surface of the globe, then man would only have four years of life left. No more bees, no more pollination, no more plants, no more animals, no more man."

THE END
You have to be careful of "the end" it might
have a stinger.

For those of you who would like to do more in-depth study of the honeybee I would greatly recommend the following websites and other documents:

- www.evolution-facts.com
- http://biology-pages.info
- "Interpreting the Symbols and Types" by Kevin J. Conner, Bible Temple Publishing
- The Dance Language and Orientation of Bees. K. von Frisch. Harvard University Press, 1967.
- The Sensory Basis of the Honeybee's Dance Language. Wolfgand H. Kirchner & William F. Towne.
- Wenner, Adrian M. and Patrick H. Wells. 1990. Anatomy of A Controversy. The Question of a "Language" Among Bees. Columbia University Press, New York.
- Frisch, Karl von. 1976 Bees: Their Vision, Chemical Senses, and Language., Cornell

University Press, Revised Edition, Ithaca N.Y.

CPSIA information can be obtained
at www.ICGtesting.com
Printed in the USA
LVOW11s1348020617
536746LV00001B/12/P